The Publishers gratefully acknowledge assistance provided by 'Gentleman' Jim Clovelly, Y.O.L.O., retirement advisor to the Retirement Advice Service (ret'd), in compiling this book.

Publishers: Ladybird Books Ltd., Loughborough

Printed in England. If wet, Italy.

'How it works'

THE
GRANDPARENT

by J.A. HAZELEY, N.S.F.W.
and J.P. MORRIS, O.M.G.

(Authors of 'What Did I Come Up Here For? –
Pensioners On Everest')

A LADYBIRD BOOK FOR GROWN–UPS

Grandparents are very versatile.

They are baby-sitters, weather forecasters, mother's helpers, sweet collectors, child-minders, knitwear suppliers, au pairs, curators of G-Plan furniture and providers of day-care for the under twelves.

Retirement is an exhausting job.

Barbara is baby-sitting her grandson, Conor.

According to her daughter's rules, Conor is allowed fifteen minutes on his iPad playing Bouncy Birds, no more.

Which leaves six hours of listening to Bobby Darin and watching old Tommy Cooper videos and whatever Barbara wants.

Every morning, Edwin takes his blood pressure pills, his statins, his anti—inflammatories, his rheumatism tablets, his glucosamine, his echinacea, his vitamins, his evening primrose oil and his zinc supplement.

Edwin wonders why he ever said no to drugs when he was at college.

He feels invincible.

"This is Molly and Pinvin in a seaside wagon," says Gloria to the man who came to fix her tap.

Gloria has so many photographs in her handbag she can barely lift it.

If a third world war wiped humanity back to a pre—digital age, Gloria could go from town to town performing as a living version of Facebook.

Since turning 60, Diane has had new teeth, an artificial hip, a plastic knee, and surgery to replace the lenses in her eyes.

As a young woman, Diane never liked doctors much, but she is a different person these days.

Probably because so many bits of her have been replaced.

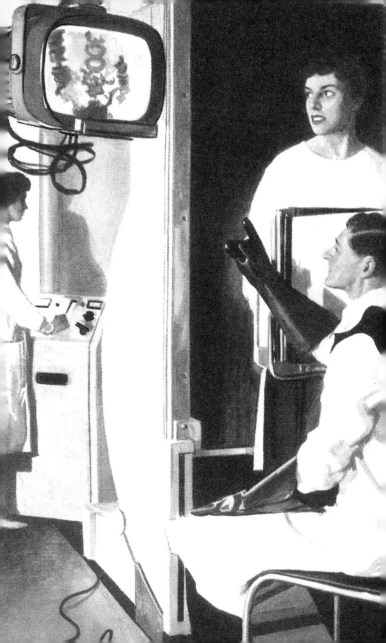

Grandparents spend a lot of time in the garden making everything tidy and pretty, so they have something tidy and pretty to look at while they are doing the gardening.

Annie and Bernard are looking after their six-month-old grand-daughter, Viola, for the first time.

"How's her weaning going?" Annie asks Viola's mum on the phone, "only I've made her a light lunch."

Linda and Derek have decorated their hallway.

Now they plan to decorate the front room, the sitting room, the bedrooms, the garage and the roof.

Then, next month, they will start on the hallway again.

All their working lives, Marie and Dennis dreamed of a retirement where they could spend a little more time together.

Unfortunately, they are spending a lot more time together, which is driving them up the wall.

Barry has taken up bell-ringing at the local church.

Barry likes bell-ringing. It drowns out the sound of his friends moaning about everything.

Before he retired, Ted worked at a nuclear power station, monitoring the pressure of the boilers and the temperature of the zirconium alloy control rods in the reactor core.

Now he does not know how to set the correct aspect ratio on his television set.

He leaves that to his nine-year-old granddaughter.

Judith is going to the doctor about her bladder pains.

On the way, she has a cup of tea at the Pavilion Tea Rooms with Steph, a cup of tea with Beatrice at the new Marks and Sparks café, a bowl of soup and a cup of tea for lunch at the Co–Op, a cup of tea at St Margaret's crypt and a cup of tea with Olive because she lives near the surgery.

"I don't know what it is, doctor," says Judith.

Lionel imagined that he'd take up golf when he retired.

In fact, he has taken up crown green bowls, because the balls are big enough to see without his glasses.

"I like to think of it as large–print snooker," he tells his grandson.

"Auntie Mary says you used to be quite a looker," says Emily to her grandfather. "When you were a looker, what did you look for?"

"Happiness," he says.

"Did you find it?" she asks.

"No," says Emily's grandfather. "I think your Auntie Mary had it all along."

Patricia calls her son-in-law in September to ask him whether he'd prefer kale or spinach with his beef on Boxing Day.

She has to know now, so she can get the veg on. Otherwise it might not be done properly.

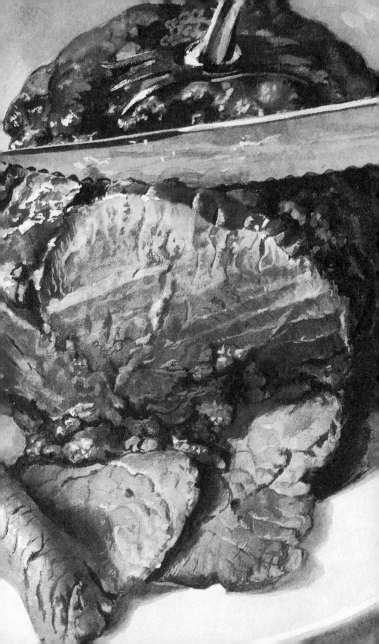

Ellie grumbles to the woman at the chemist's that Gordon has lost his get–up–and–go.

Gordon thinks that if Ellie still shared his bed, she'd know that every night at 4am, he has to get up and go, regular as clockwork.

Angela is in Age Concern buying yet more DVDs that came free with the Mail on Sunday.

"They're a bargain, these," says Angela. "And better than the rubbish on television."

Angela will put them in the cupboard with the others. She does not really watch films.

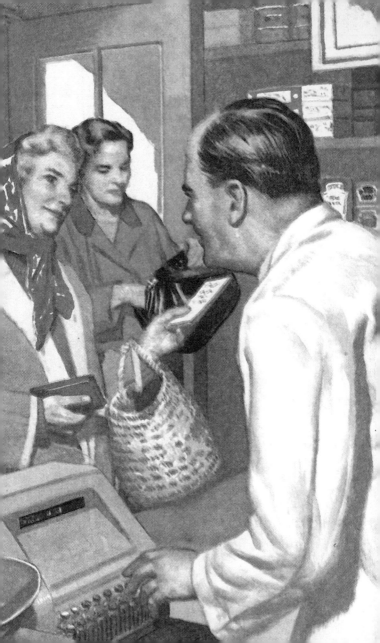

Maureen's granddaughter has a gluten allergy, a nut allergy, and an egg allergy.

Maureen's cake only contains a couple of ounces of flour, a little bit of walnut and just the one egg, so she is sure her grand-daughter will be fine with it.

"Is your heating working, Dad?" Rachel asks her 86-year-old father.

"Yes, dear," he says. "I've set the thermostat to fourteen degrees."

Rachel's dad says he doesn't feel the cold. He is wearing eleven cardigans and five tea cosies. He can't even feel the chair he's in.

Janet is always popular with her fellow rotarians because she has gin stashed all over town.

Bill is telling his grandchildren about the time his band opened for The Sex Pistols.

Noah asks his grandfather which came first — The Sex Pistols or the dinosaurs?

These mail—order factory—made heirlooms have been designed to appeal to grandparents.

They cost £99.99 in monthly instalments, but will be worth much more to the grandchildren who inherit them.

Or 50p to the Sue Ryder shop.

Don used to tell his grandchildren tall tales about all the adventures he would have if he owned a boat.

Don's annuity matured this year.

"The kids would love a go on your boat," yells Don's daughter.

"Can't hear you," Don shouts back at the quayside.

"I don't know what you're all standing there for," says Nigel.

"I've spent the lot."